Easy Classical Piano Duets

Compiled and arranged by Taeko Hirao

Contents

Order No. AM 31949
International Standard Book Number: 978.0.8256.2173.9
Library of Congress Catalog Card Number: 76-51891

Turkish March

Secondo

Ludwig van Beethoven
(1770-1827)

Allegretto

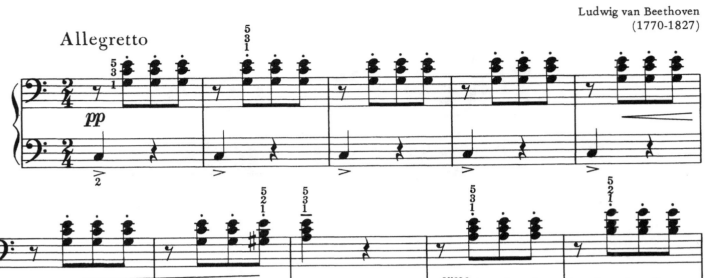

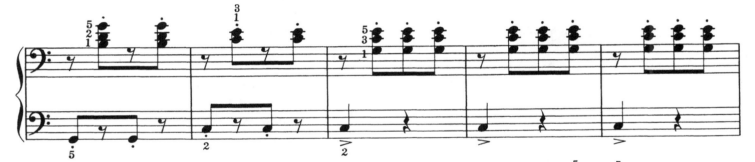

Turkish March

Primo

Ludwig van Beethoven
(1770-1827)

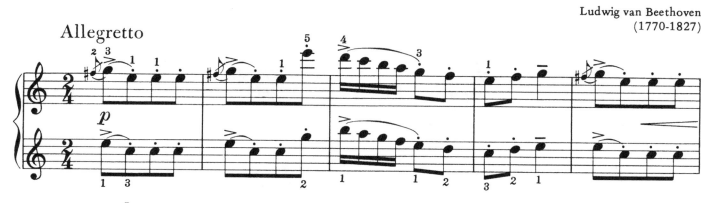

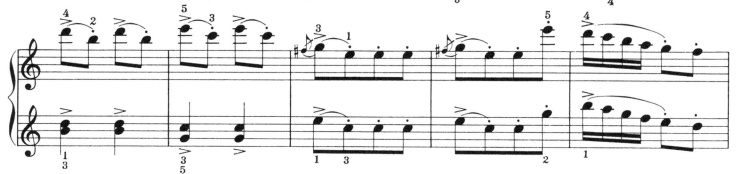

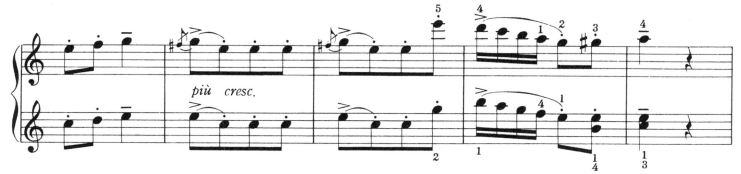

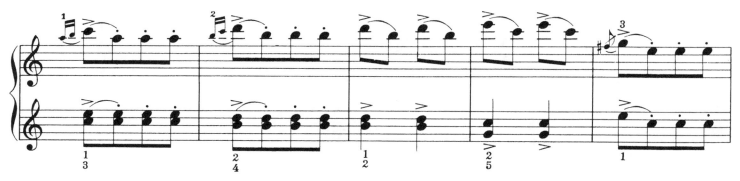

Secondo

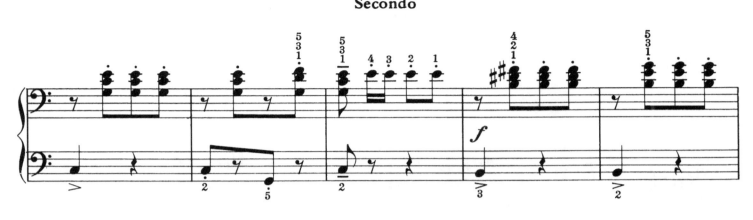

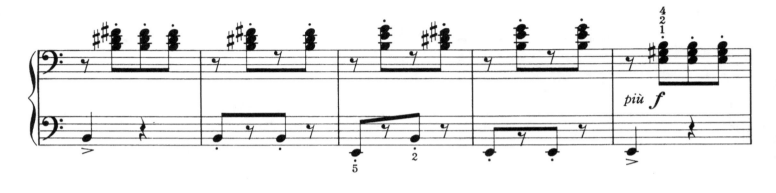

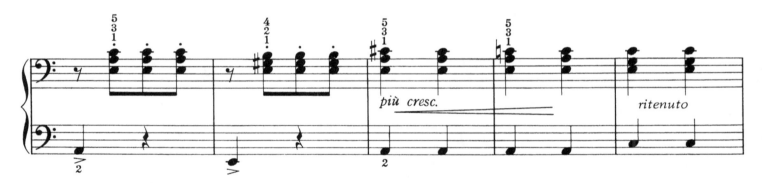

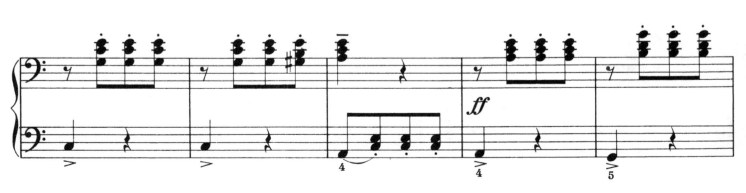

4

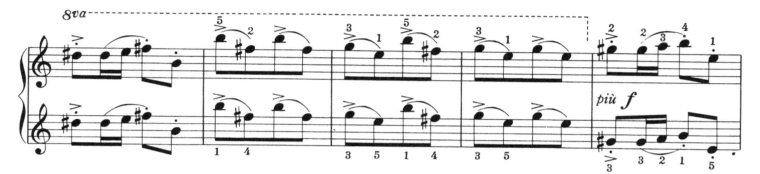

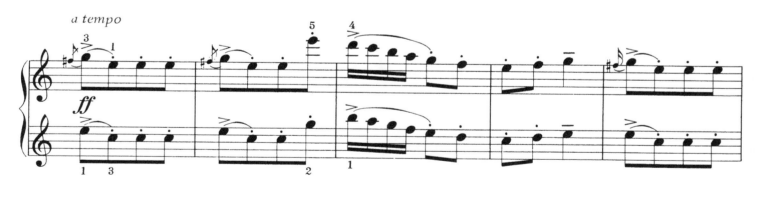

Secondo

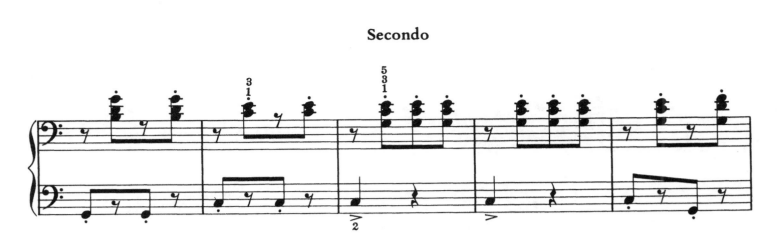

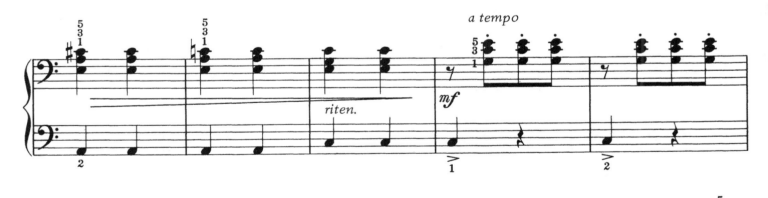

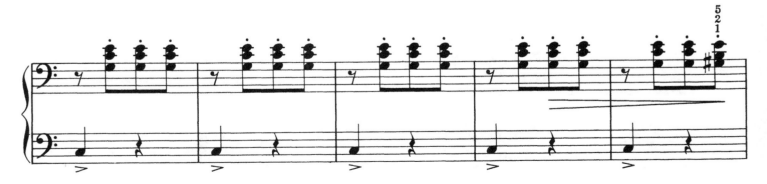

Primo

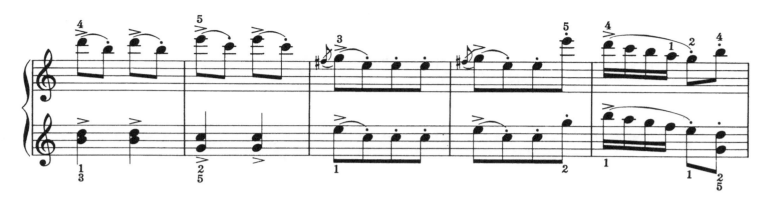

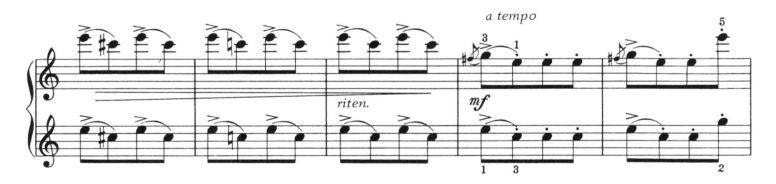

7

Secondo

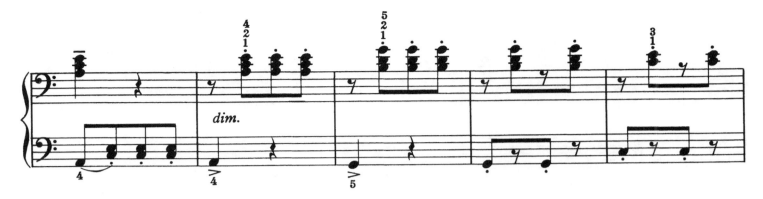

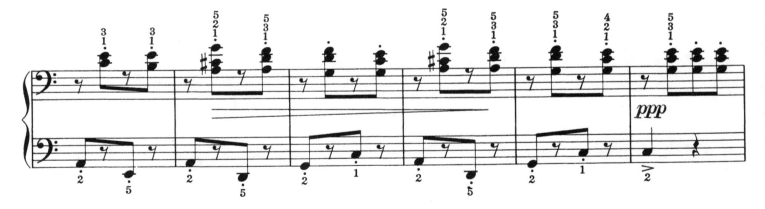

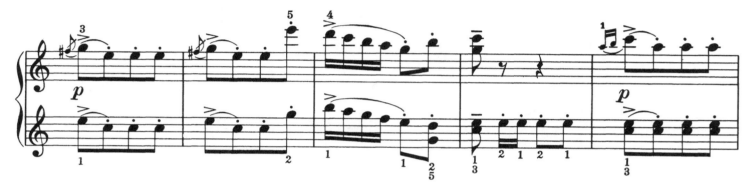

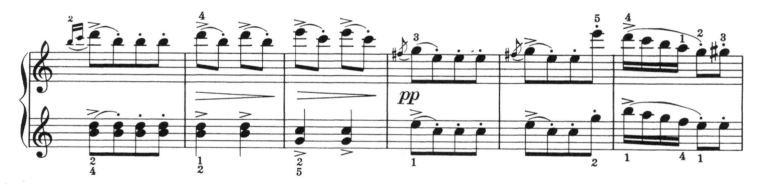

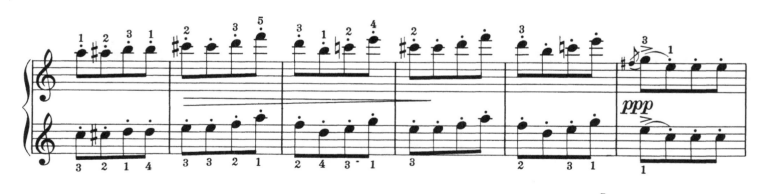

Marche Militaire

Secondo

Franz Schubert
(1797-1828)

Allegro Vivace

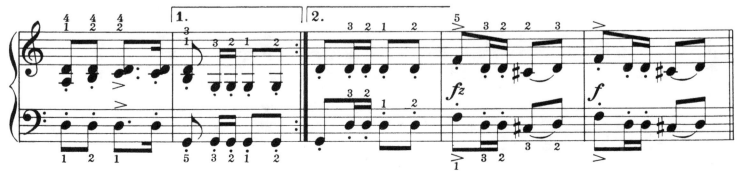

Marche Militaire

Primo

Franz Schubert
(1797-1828)

Secondo

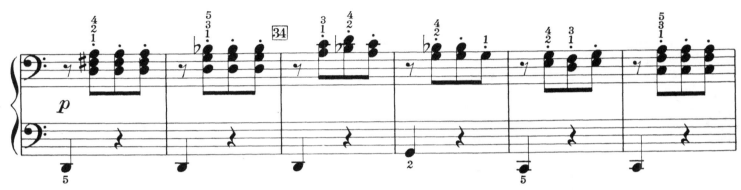

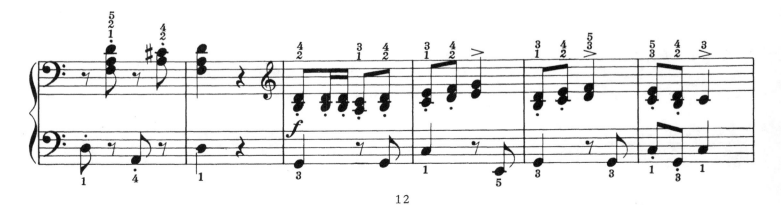

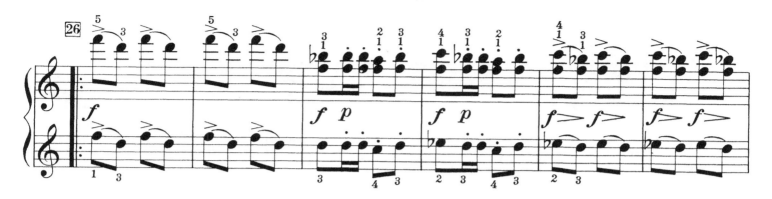

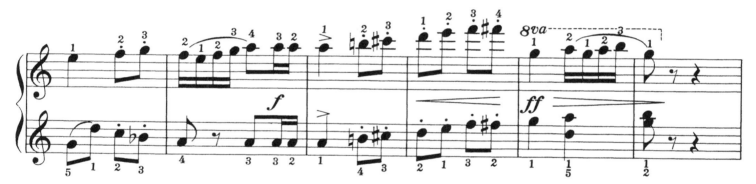

Primo

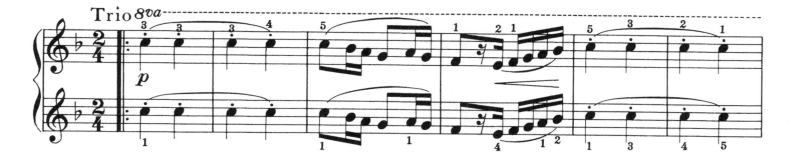

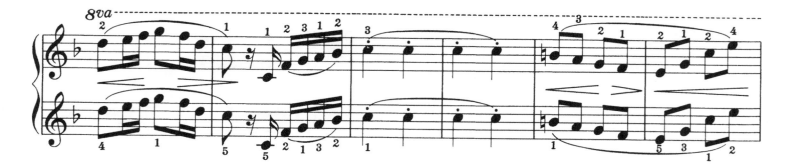

Secondo

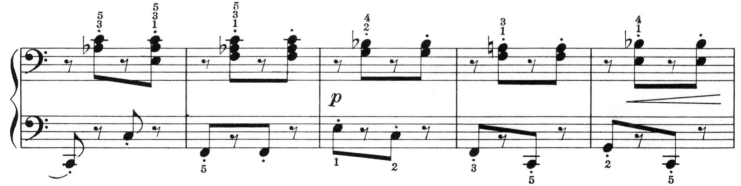

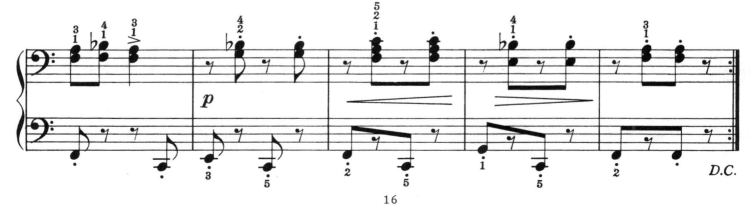

D.C.

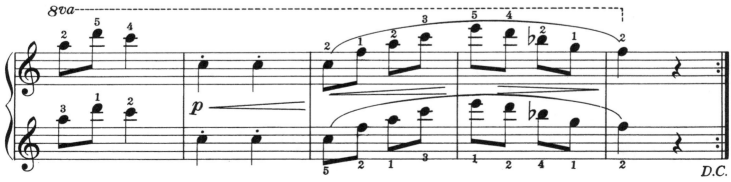

D.C.

Czech Polka

Secondo

Johann Strauss II
(1825-1899)

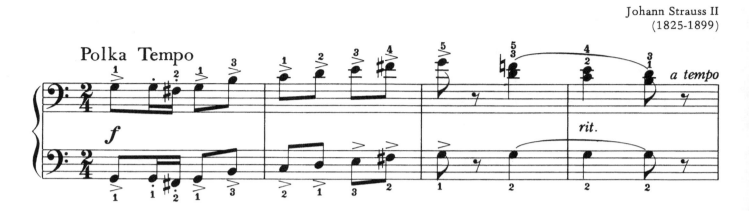

Czech Polka

Primo

Johann Strauss II
(1825-1899)

Secondo

Trio

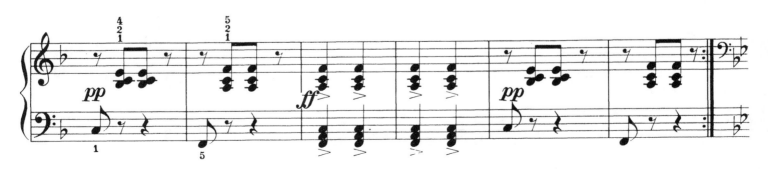

Trio

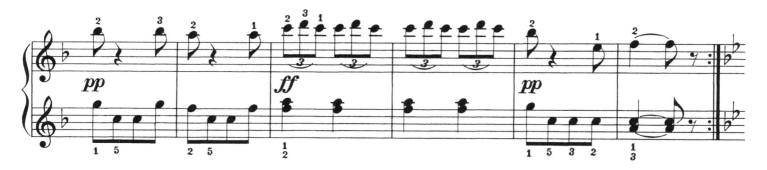

Secondo

Primo

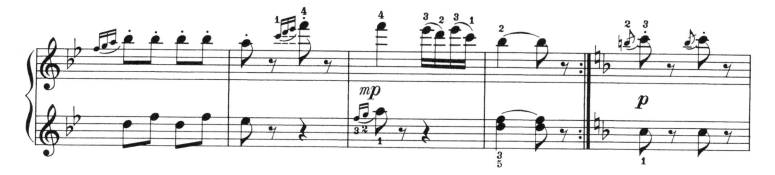

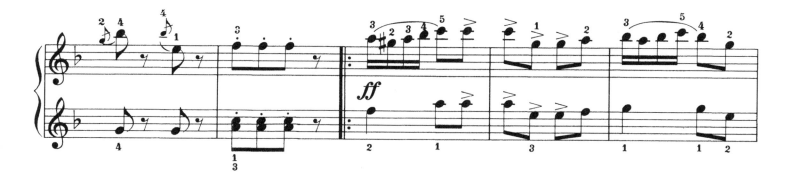

23

Secondo

Secondo

Primo

Annen Polka

(Anna Polka)

Secondo

Johann Strauss II
(1825-1899)

Allegretto

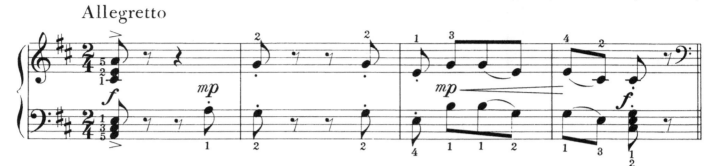

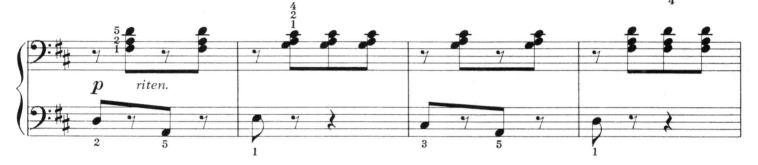

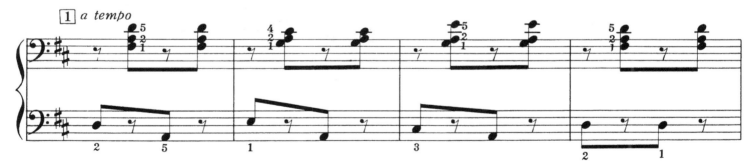

Annen Polka

(Anna Polka)

Primo

Johann Strauss II
(1825-1899)

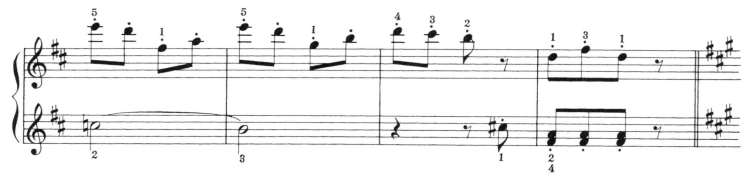

Secondo

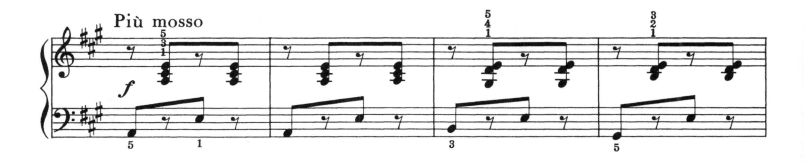

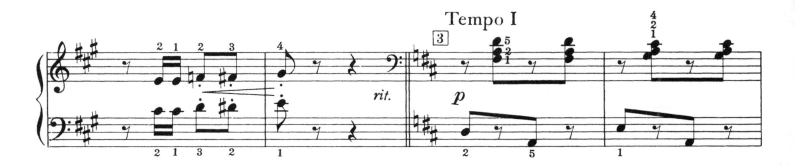

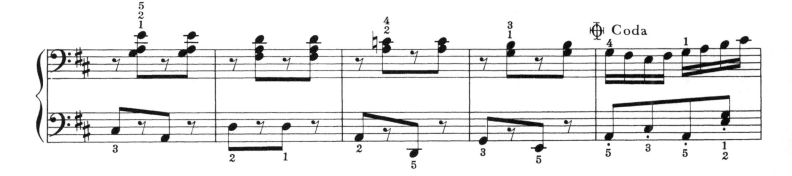

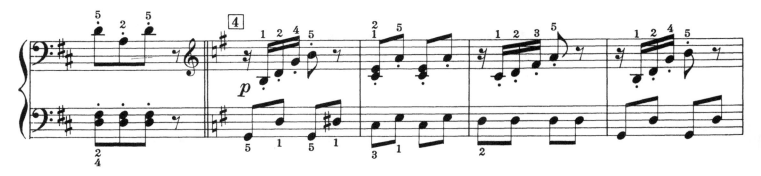

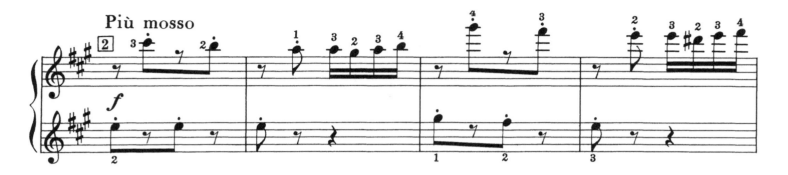

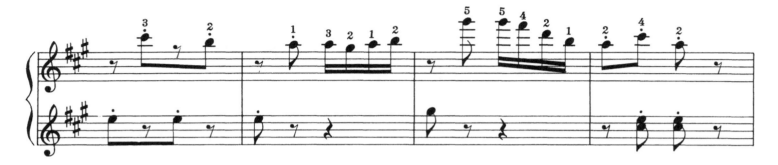

Secondo

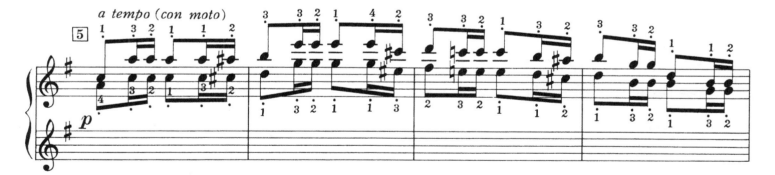

Secondo

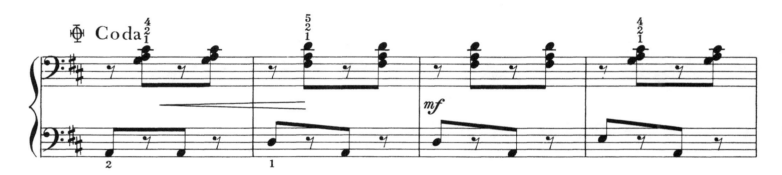

Vivace

D.C.

Coda

Norwegian Dance

Secondo

Edvard Grieg
(1843-1907)

Allegro tranquillo e grazioso (♩ = 76)

Norwegian Dance

Primo

Edvard Grieg
(1843-1907)

Allegro (♩ = 112)

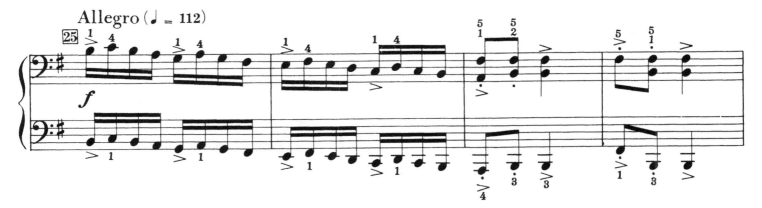

Secondo

March of the Dwarfs

Secondo

Edvard Grieg
(1843-1907)

Allegro moderato

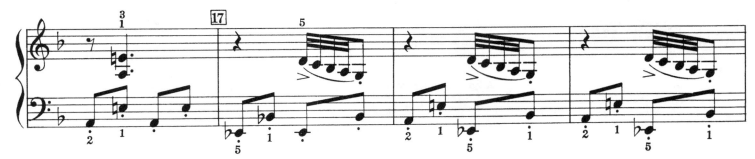

March of the Dwarfs

Primo

Edvard Grieg
(1843-1907)

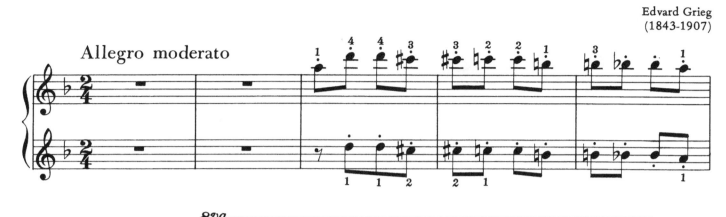

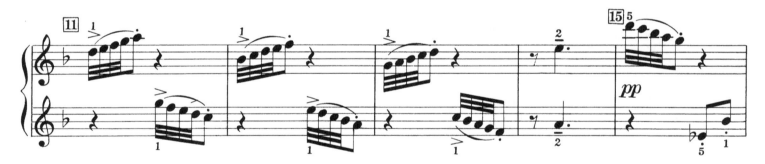

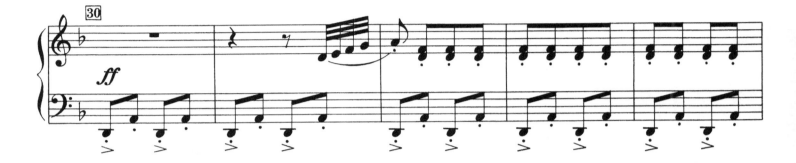

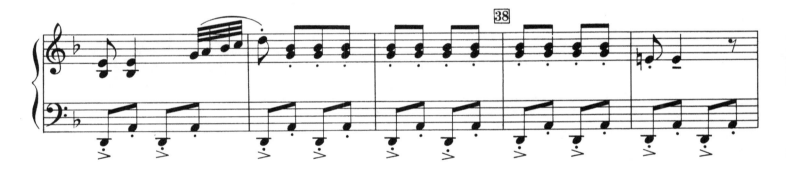

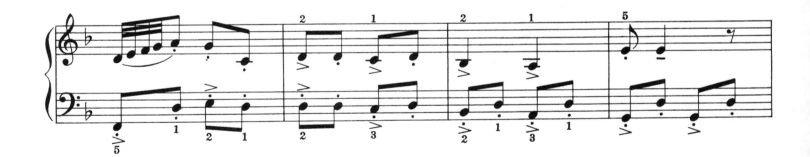

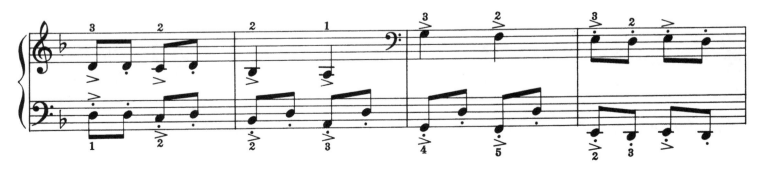

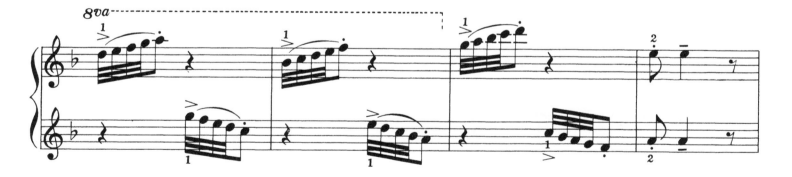

Secondo

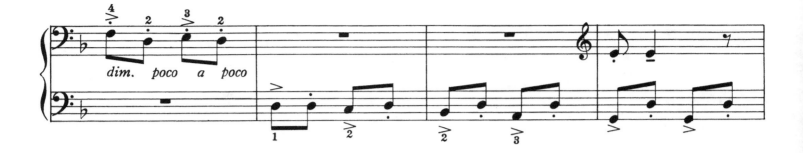

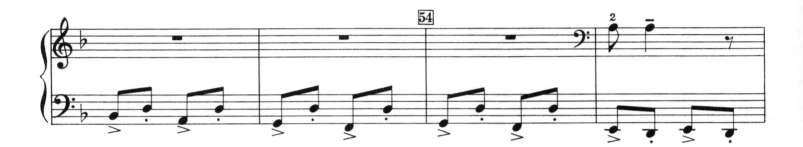

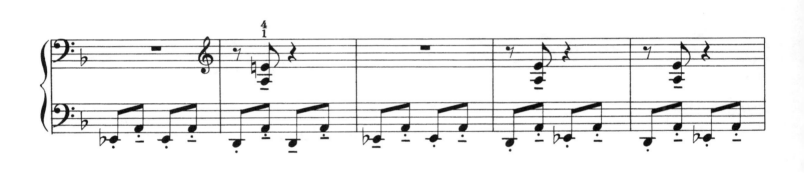

Primo

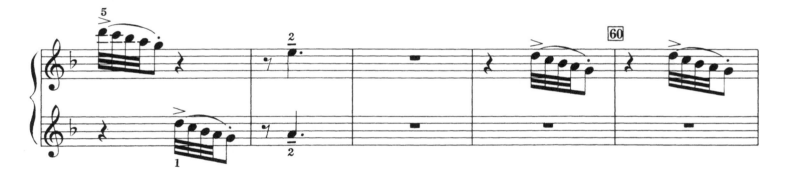

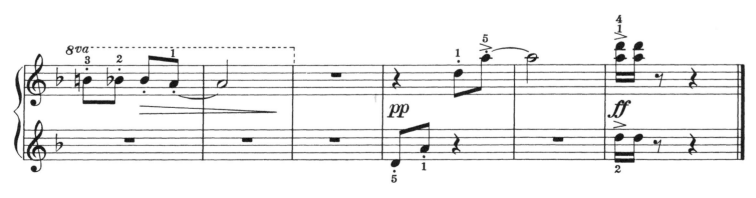

47

Pizzicatto Polka

Secondo

Johann Strauss II (1825-1899) and
Josef Strauss (1827-1870)

Pizzicatto Polka

Primo

Johann Strauss II (1825-1899) and
Josef Strauss (1827-1870)

Secondo

𝄋 al ⊕ Coda

Trio

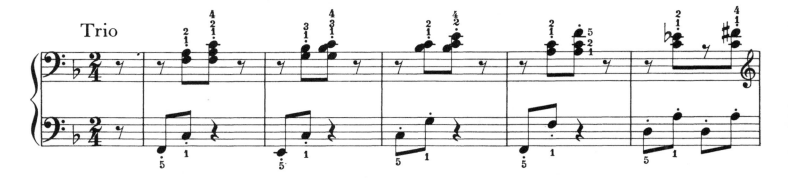

50

% al⊕ Coda

Trio

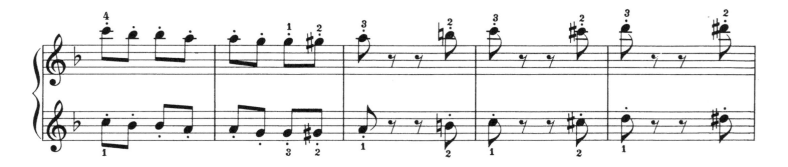

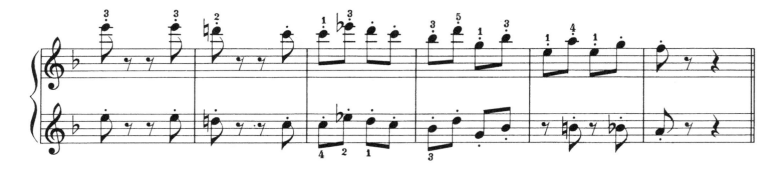

D.C. al 𝄋
e poi la Coda

✛ Coda
Piu Allegro

D.C. al ℅
e poi la Coda

⊕ Coda
Piu Allegro

Radetzky March

Secondo

Johann Strauss I
(1804-1849)

Allegro Moderato

Radetzky March

Primo

Johann Strauss I
(1804-1849)

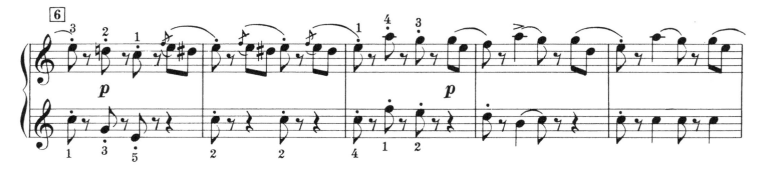

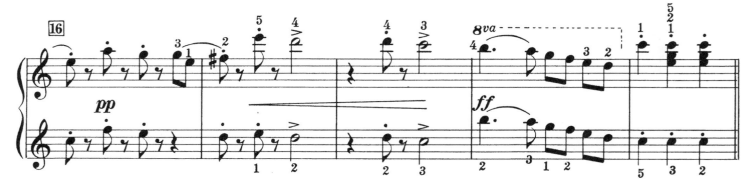

Secondo

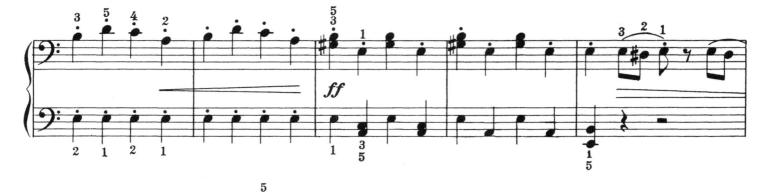

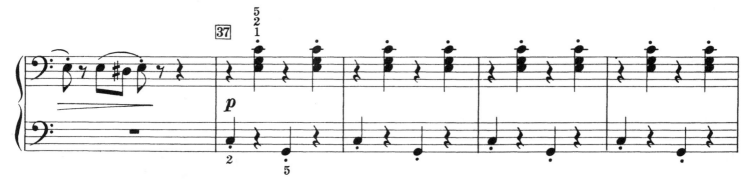

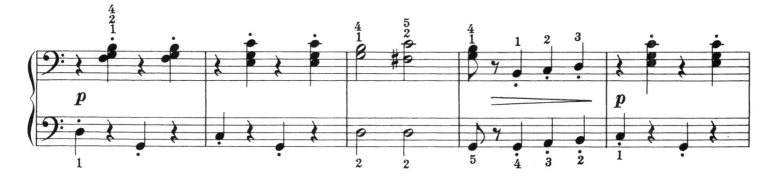

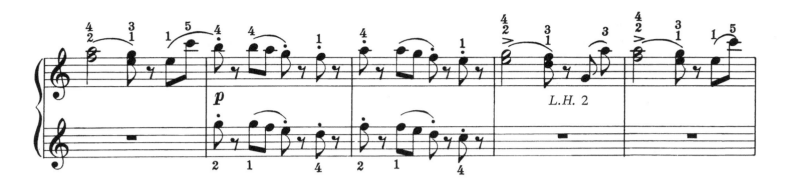

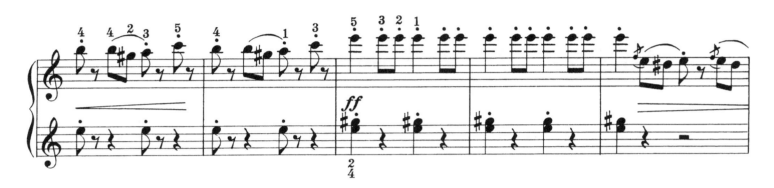

Secondo

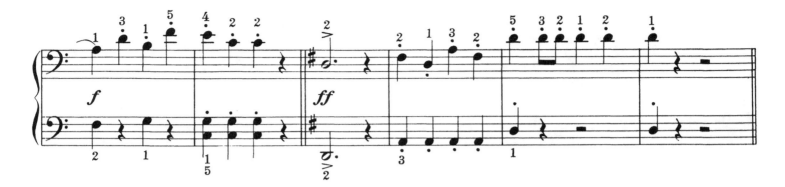

Trio

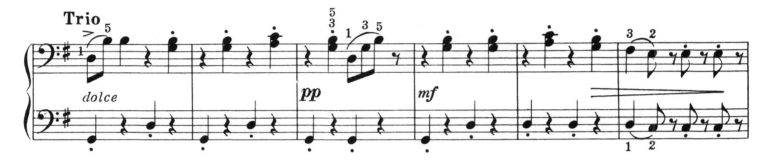

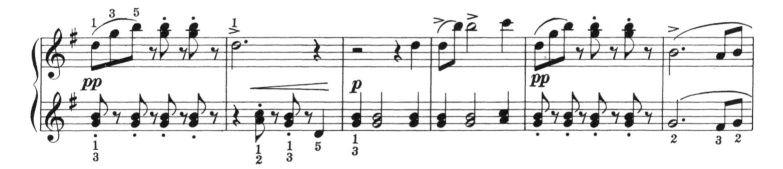

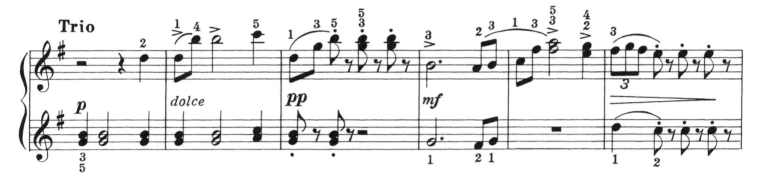

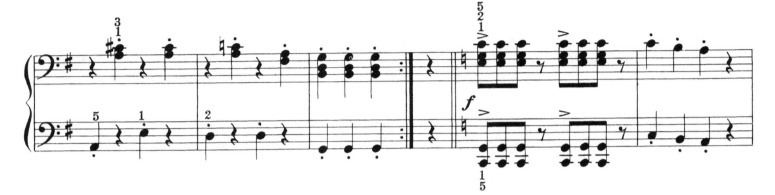

Primo

Secondo

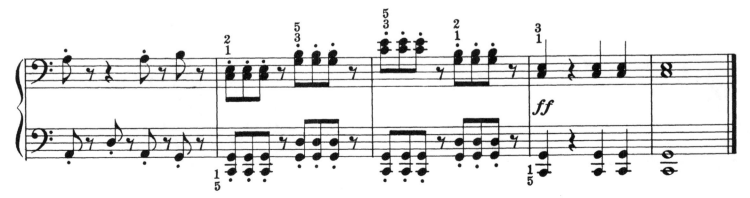

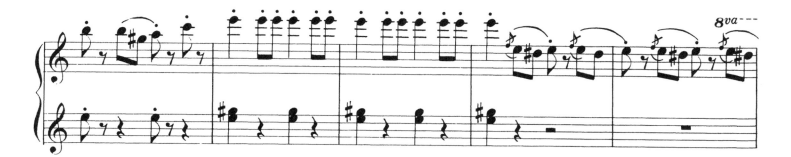

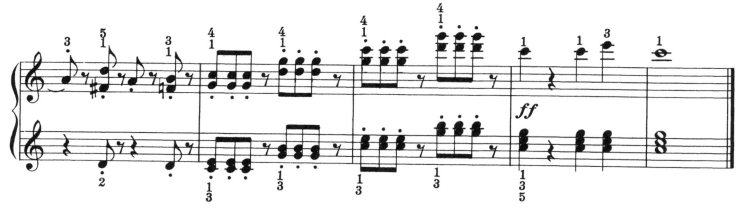